BE STRONG

& *Courageous*

Journal For Men with Inspirational Quotes
&
Words of Encouragement
(7 x 10 Inches)

This Journal Belongs To:

www.InspirationalWares.com

HABIT/GOAL TRACKER

Start Date:

Habit/Goal	1	2	3	4	5	6	7	8	9	10	11	12	13	14	15	16	17	18	19	20	21	22	23	24	25

Date:

Date:

Hope is the only thing stronger than fear.

Date:

Don't let the behavior of others destroy inner peace.

If you can't stop thinking about it, don't stop working for it.

Date:

Date:

Trust yourself. You know more than you think you do. - Ben Spock

If you're lucky enough to be different, don't ever change.

Date:

If you have never failed you have never lived.

Date:

Faith can move mountains.

Date:

When life knocks you down, try to land on your back. Because if you can look up, you can get up. – Les Brown

Date:

Date:

Keep your face always toward the sunshine—and shadows will fall behind you. - Walt Whitman

Date:

This too shall pass.

Date:

What the caterpillar calls the end of the world, the master calls a butterfly.

Date:

Date:

Everything you can imagine is real. - Pablo Picasso

Date:

Date:

The game is won in the mind.

Go as long as you can, and then take another step.

Date:

Worry does not empty tomorrow of its sorrow, it empties today of its strength.

A word of encouragement during a failure is worth more than an hour of praise after success.

Date:

Date:

Stop wearing your wishbone where your backbone ought to be.

Enjoy the little things.

Date:

Date:

God brings men into deap waters not to drown them, but to cleanse them.

Date:

Date:

Date:

Date:

I've never met a strong person with an easy part.

Date:

A strong soul shines after every storm.

Date:

Believe in yourself a little more.

Turn your wounds into wisdom. - Oprah Winfrey

Date:

Beginnings are always messy. - John Galsworth

Date:

It's hard to beat someone who never gives up.

Date:

You can and you will.

What would you do if you weren't afraid?

Date:

It is not the mountain we conquer, but ourselves. - Edmund Hillary

Date:

Date:

Work hard, stay humble.

Date:

How others see you is unimportant. How you see yourself means everything.

Date:

Learn from yesterday, live for today, hope for tomorrow.

The secret of having it all is believing you already do.

Don't let anyone ever break your soul.

Date:

Date:

Life shrinks or expands in proportion to one's courage.

Date:

I am what I choose to become.

Date:

Date:

You are stronger than you think.

Date:

What's done is done. - William Shakespeare

Date:

Date:

It is never too late to be what you might have been.

Date:

Change your thoughts and you change your world. – Norman Vincent Peale

Date:

We all have a fighter in us.

Date:

Date:

You have to be at your strongest when you're feeling at your weakest.

We all have limits. Almost no one reaches theirs.

Date:

Date:

Never let the odds keep you from doing what you know in your heart you were meant to do.

The art of living lies less in eliminating our troubles than with growing with them.

Date:

Be strong and courageous.

If you can dream it, you can achieve it. – Zig Ziglar

If the wind will not serve, take to the oars.

GOAL ACTION PLANS

"

A nail is driven out by another nail. Habit is overcome by habit.

"

- Desiderius Erasmus

...re: **Date Accomplished:**

To Establish:

>

Motivation:

>

Progress:

(1) (2) (3) (4) (5) (6) (7) (8) (9) (10) (11) (12) (13) (14) (15)

(16) (17) (18) (19) (20) (21) (22) (23) (24) (25) (26) (27) (28) (29) (30)

(31)

Reward:

>

Start Date: **Date Accomplished:**

Habit To Establish:

>

Motivation:

>

Progress:

(1) (2) (3) (4) (5) (6) (7) (8) (9) (10) (11) (12) (13) (14) (15)

(16) (17) (18) (19) (20) (21) (22) (23) (24) (25) (26) (27) (28) (29) (30)

(31)

Reward:

>

Start Date: **Date Accomplished:**

Habit To Establish:

Motivation:

Progress:

(1) (2) (3) (4) (5) (6) (7) (8) (9) (10) (11) (12) (13) (14) (15)

(16) (17) (18) (19) (20) (21) (22) (23) (24) (25) (26) (27) (28) (29) (30)

(31)

Reward:

Start Date: **Date Accomplished:**

Habit To Establish:

Motivation:

Progress:

(1) (2) (3) (4) (5) (6) (7) (8) (9) (10) (11) (12) (13) (14) (15)

(16) (17) (18) (19) (20) (21) (22) (23) (24) (25) (26) (27) (28) (29) (30)

(31)

Reward:

e: Date Accomplished:
    Io Establish:

>

Motivation:

>

Progress:

(1) (2) (3) (4) (5) (6) (7) (8) (9) (10) (11) (12) (13) (14) (15)

(16) (17) (18) (19) (20) (21) (22) (23) (24) (25) (26) (27) (28) (29) (30)

(31)

Reward:

>

Start Date: **Date Accomplished:**
Habit To Establish:

>

Motivation:

>

Progress:

(1) (2) (3) (4) (5) (6) (7) (8) (9) (10) (11) (12) (13) (14) (15)

(16) (17) (18) (19) (20) (21) (22) (23) (24) (25) (26) (27) (28) (29) (30)

(31)

Reward:

>

For more amazing journals and adult coloring books from Penelope Pewter, visit:

Amazon.com
CNandJ.com
InspirationalWares.com

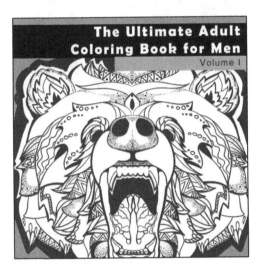

The Ultimate Adult Coloring Book for Men

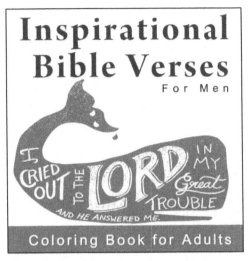

Inspirational Bible Verses for Men
Coloring Book for Adults

Surf's Up Dude
The Adult Coloring Book

The Adult Coloring Book for Coffee Lovers

Be Strong

Be Courageous

Support comes in many forms (purchases, likes, Amazon reviews). We truly appreciate all the support our patrons have provided us. As a "Thank You" for your continuing support and as a token of our appreciation, below is an QR Code for you to download a **free** "Be Strong" and "Be Courageous" printable PDF files - 8x10*:

How to scan a QR code from an iPhone or iPad

- Open the Camera app from on your iPhone or iPad.
- Make sure the rear facing camera is selected.
- Position your device to take a photo of the QR code.
- Center the QR code in the viewfinder (your device should recognize the QR code and display a message).
- Tap the notification to download your PDF.

For Personal Use Only

Made in the USA
Columbia, SC
14 December 2022

73823711R00063